Visualizati

MW01298029

Creative Visualization Techniques And Visualization Meditation Guide To Achieve Goals And Optimal Mindset Success!

Ryan Cooper

STOP!!! Before you read any further....Would you like to know the Success Secrets of how to make Passive Income Online?

If your answer is yes, then you are not alone. Thousands of people are looking for the secret to learning how to create their own online passive income style business.

If you have been searching for these answers without much luck, you are in the right place!

Because I want to make sure to give you as much value as possible for purchasing this book, right now for a limited time you can get 3 incredible bonuses for free.

At the end of this book I describe all 3 bonuses. You can access them at the end. But for those of you that want to grab your bonuses right now. See below.

Just Go Here For Free Instant Access:

www.OperationAwesomeLife.com/FreeBonuses

Legal Notice

Disclaimer Notice

Table Of Contents

Introduction

I want to thank you and congratulate you for purchasing the book, *Visualization Techniques - Creative Visualization Techniques And Visualization Meditation Guide To Achieve Goals And Optimal Mindset Success*!

This book contains insight on how you can design your life through proper visualization in regards to your individual life blueprint.

Do you know what you want most in life? If so, you are on the right track! Now you need to learn the proper way to draw a blueprint for your plan on paper and most importantly, in your mind.

If you want to build a hotel, a golf course, a car, or simply a house, you would need one thing - a vision of what you want to build, and a plan to build it.

Reaching for your goals is much the same. Just as you would need a great architect to build a fine building, you need to be the architect of your own life. You need to be armed with the understanding of how to visualize what you want, and also to understand how to obtain plans for your endeavor. This book will serve as a reference to mind architecture and how you can use it.

Thanks again for purchasing this book, I hope you enjoy it!

Chapter 1: Visualization - How Can It Help You Succeed

Visualization is creating images in your mind of you doing or having something that you want, and repeating them over and over again. It is a mental trick that allows you to feel and live the images you create in your brain as if they are actually happening. For example, you can imagine yourself being the successful person that you want, heal the illness that has been bothering you for a while, being able to close an important deal or having a great relationship. You can do your visualization every day for five minutes.

Visualization is not about hoping that someday, what you aspire will happen or that it will build your confidence so that you can fulfill your goals someday. You visualize in your mind that you already have what you want and you are already living the life that you have always dreamt of. Although you are aware at one level that visualization is a mental trick, your subconscious cannot distinguish between imagination and reality. It acts upon the images that you create within your mind. It doesn't matter if these images are the reflection of your current reality or not.

To achieve your goal, visualization can help by:

- Allowing you to become consciously aware of the things that can help you achieve your desired outcome by visualizing it over and over again in your mind. Visualization helps you get rid of anything that does not correspond to the image that you are visualizing. Continuously visualizing your desired outcome in your mind involves all the cells in your body to that image and you mirror and reverberate with everything that goes in harmony with that frequency, both in the physical and non-physical level. This frequency lets you move towards everything that you need in order to manifest your desired image.

- Letting you impress your desired idea to your subconscious mind which eventually becomes fixed so that your body automatically moves toward and attract whatever you desire. Athletes use visualization because they are conditioning their mind so that their bodies will act the way they wanted them to without exerting much effort. Visualization allows a person to become unconsciously competent wherein competence becomes a natural part of your being. This idea works the same with successful people. These people repeats their desired outcome in their minds over and over again until their bodies automatically does whatever is needed to turn their dreams into a physical reality.

The mind is very powerful. It is the tool that helps you understand the world that you live in. Through visualization, you are able to experience your dreams even before it becomes a physical reality. It allows you to get a taste of your desired outcome which helps stimulate your burning desire to turn it into a reality. Focusing intently on something that you desire for yourself allows you to feel the emotions that you would feel in the actual event, allowing you to live the moment before it becomes a reality.

When you stay true to yourself and you visualize the best future for you, this future will spark a burning desire within you and if you properly feed it, will continually burn until your dreams become a reality. Visualizing your desired future over and over again will make you want it so dearly that you will do everything to turn it into reality.

Visualization allows you to focus on your desired future and helps you determine the things that can help you to turn this dream into a reality. Visualization moves you towards your dream wherein you automatically do what is necessary to manifest your dream into a physical reality.

Chapter 2: How To Accomplish Your Plans Through Visualization

Creative visualization is a mental trick that uses imagination to make one's dreams come true. Through creative visualization, you will be able to attract prosperity and success. It gives you the power to alter your circumstances and your environment, attract work, possessions, money, people and love in your life and make events happen. Creative visualization reaps the benefits of the power of the mind, a very powerful tool that is behind every success.

What you think about can come true. Visualization is not changing anything material. Through visualization, you change your thoughts which in turn changes the way you shape your life. But not all thoughts do come true, only those that are concentrated upon, repeated over and over and well-defined; hence, the importance of the vision board.

The vision board is simply a poster board wherein you stick images you've collected to constantly remind you of the person you want to become, the place you want to live at, the car you want to own and whatever it is that you desire. There are 5 simple ways of creating your own vision board:

- Collect as much magazines that you can find and start looking for words, phrases and images that strike you most. You don't have to be serious about it. Just let yourself have fun and get as much images as you can.

- Now, go through the images that you got from your magazines. This is where you sort out your chosen images.

Retain the images that you like and discard those that does not appeal to you anymore. This way, you get to form a lay out of how you want your visual board to look like. You may want to assign a theme on each side of your visual board such as love,

- success, health and love. You may also want to just place the images all over or create a book that tells your story through the images.

- Glue the images you have chosen into your visual board. You can be artistic with it to make it more appealing. You can add some paint or write some words using colorful markers, whatever it is that pleases you.

- Leave a space on the very center of your vision board and paste a picture of yourself . Choose a picture wherein you are happy and radiant. This will keep reminding you to stay positive and your dreams are soon to be a reality.

- Place your vision board somewhere noticeable, where you can see it all the time.

Your vision board will keep reminding you of your dream and will help fuel that burning desire inside you to manifest your dreams into a physical reality.

There are three types of visions boards:

1. I know what I want

   You can create this board if you are clear with what you desire in life, there is a change you want to happen in your surroundings or environment and you want something specific to happen in your life. For example, you want a new house or you want to own a brand new Mercedes Benz.

How to create this board:

- Look for pictures that exactly portray your vision. If you want a new Mercedes Benz, look for a picture of that car with the exact color and model. If you want a house with a grand garden, choose a

- picture that illustrates your ideal home. If it is a business that you desire, cut out pictures that capture your ideas.

- After choosing your desired pictures, just follow the steps outlined above and create your "I know what I want" vision board.

2. Opening and Allowing

This vision board is ideal for those who are not exactly sure of what they want. This is also ideal for those who just underwent depression or a period of grief. There are also those who know what they want but are not sure about it in some ways or those who want change but are not certain how to do it. The "opening and allowing" vision board is ideal for these people.

How to create this board:

- Go through your magazines and tear out the pictures that make you happy. It does not matter if it's a flower or a doll that made you smile. Just have fun with choosing your images.

- Sort out the images that you collected from your magazines. This time, ask yourself, what does this image mean to me? Does this flower mean I have to let go of negative people that drains me? Does this doll mean anything to me? Most likely, you have the answer, but if you don't and you still love the picture and it strikes you, pin it on your vision board. You will have the answer eventually.

The "opening and allowing" vision board is a powerful visualization tool. It does not only help you get what you want, it also tells you more about your passion and yourself.

3. Theme

This vision board is ideal for you if you are working on a specific area of your life such as career or work or if there is a significant event in your life that starts a new cycle like New Year's Eve or your birthday.

How to create this board:

- Before you begin to select the images that you will stick on your vision board, you must clearly visualize in your mind the intent and theme of your vision board.

- Choose pictures and images that are in alignment to your theme and intent.

The only difference of the Theme vision board from the first two is that it has specific parameters and intent.

You can create a combination of these vision boards if you may. You can start with creating one type of vision board and as you go along, your vision board might change depending on what mode your intuition takes you.

Vision boards are a great visualization tool because the mind cannot distinguish from what is contrived and what is real and the brain thinks in pictures. The vision board is a powerful complement to the declarations you've started on your morning rituals and evening practices of gratitude.

You may also create a vision journal which employs the same principles used in the vision board using a large sketch book. This can be very helpful when you are going through a lot of transitions in your life.

Chapter 3: Your Visual Blueprint To Success

Success has different meanings by different people. You have to know what you desire for yourself. In order to get to where you want to be, here is a visualization blueprint that you can use to help you achieve your dreams.

- Write down what you desire. Sit down on a quiet place with your pen and paper and write down the outcome that you want. By doing so, you make a physical commitment to it and hold on firmly to that commitment. If you want to put up a new business or create a new product, write it down and stay firmly committed to it.

- Break down your goal into smaller, measurable tasks. Since you already know your end goal, it is now easier to break it down into smaller goals. For example, if you want to create a new product, you may break down your goal into smaller tasks such as these:

  - Marketing research or niche marketing

  - Gathering online and offline information for the product content

  - Creating a product video

  - Producing the product video

  - Uploading the video to your site

- Make a schedule for completing your tasks. Get your calendar and map out your schedule for every task. You do not want to be burnt out so you should not push yourself too much. In the example above, you may start your marketing/niche research at 9am on Monday and spend an hour on it before you move on to your next task. When you give yourself specific timeframes, your mind will rise up to the challenge.

- Visualize your success every day. Take 5 minutes each day to stay in a quiet place and visualize your success. Think about how it will make you feel when you achieve it, how your life will be different. You don't have to spend too much time on it. Visualize yourself doing the tasks and finishing them on time every day with little effort. Your mind is a very powerful tool, make use of it.

- Reward yourself when you complete a task. Rewarding yourself each time you complete a task reaffirms your end goal and it also makes you feel good. You can reward yourself with simple things such as a 10 minute walk at the park or an ice cream treat. Do something about your success, even how small it is, it gives you a sense of fulfillment.

- Success achieved. Now that you have achieved your end goal, you are ready to move on to the next one. Stacking your achievements help you achieve bigger and bigger success. The more successes you achieve, the more your momentum is fueled up. Your success is driven by your momentum. The more you achieve, the bigger successes you attract.

Chapter 4: Key Points In Visualization

Visualization helps you create your own reality and achieve your desired success in life. Here are key points in visualization that will help you manifest your dreams into a physical reality.

- The pictures that you create in your mind have an impact your life and the actions that you take.

- When you visualize, you activate the parts of your brain that is responsible for carrying out your actions.

- The subconscious mind is excellent when it comes to reverse engineering due to its deductive nature. It can work wonderfully backwards going to the means.

- If you focus intently on a single goal in your mind, your subconscious will automatically help you find the means and information that are needed to achieve your goal.

- You don't necessarily need to know how to get to your goal. Your subconscious mind will help you with that.

- It is important and necessary that you are able to feel and see your goal as if it already happened when you visualize it.

Many successful people have used this technique either consciously or unconsciously. When using visualization to achieve your goal, remember to be clear with your intention, avoid any distractions and experience your intention or ultimate goal as if it already happened or it is already a done deal.

Chapter 5: Improve Your Self-Image Using Visualization Technique

This visualization technique is very helpful especially when you are feeling down and starting to lose hope on yourself.

The Magic Mirror

Imagine that you are in an empty room with a table. On the table, there is a double-sided mirror and you reached for it. As you look in the mirror, it looks normal but there is something special about it. You looked at the mirror and saw yourself as a beautiful, capable and a powerful person. You see in the mirror the person that you ought to be.

You Are Wonderful

As you continue looking at the mirror, you start feeling wonderful about yourself as the mirror also reveals the true beauty inside you. It makes you feel genuine excitement believing that you are actually powerful and beautiful. As you look into the mirror, you are able to accept your virtues and your talents and you start to believe in yourself naturally.

The magic mirror also lets you see deep inside you. It allows you to see your life experiences and lessons and how they are being reorganized so that you can show off your skill, talent and knowledge. Now you see how you can make use of these experiences and turn them into wealth and beauty which is powerful and pure.

You Are Powerful

As you continue to look at your inner beauty, you come to understand that all the answers you've been seeking are inside you and have always been there. As you look at your reflected beauty, power, talents and skills and how much you are loved by God, you realize that you will never be afraid again. Now you realize that whenever you are confronted with a difficult situation in your life, all you need to do is look in the magic mirror and take a look at your life and the answers to your questions will be given to you. You will be directed to the right person, the right information and right solution all the time. You come to realize that this is already inside of you and you already know how to access it after seeing it in the magic mirror.

As you look into your magic mirror, you began to realize that everything you need in your life, to make you powerful, healthy, fulfilled and financially-free is all waiting for you. Everything you need is inside you now. The magic mirror shows you that it was always there for you to use, you just didn't have the mirror before.

As you keep looking at the mirror, you start to feel comfortable and warm inside. Now you are able to see all the resources that you can use in life. Now you know that everything you need is already within you and all you need to do is look at yourself in the magic mirror, accept it, and it will be yours. Now you realize that you have a better future and it makes you smile.

You Are A Leader

As you continue to look at your magic mirror, you notice that there are other magic mirrors. You realize that you can share a magic mirror with anyone you want to. You can share a magic mirror with anyone who wants to see deep within them, realize their own power and see life as it really is.

As you look deeply into the mirror, you see this person who has always been mean and negative to you, walk inside the room. As you are enjoying your wonderful experiences, this negative person starts saying bad things to you but you can't hear them. You realize that the words of the negative person are bouncing off of your magic mirror and the words are thrown back into his throat. His words are fast disappearing so you cannot hear them.

Your magic mirror is also your shield. From now on, you no longer have to listen to the negative comments of people around you. No negative person can ever again put you off guard, hurt you or distract you. No one can ever take you away from your internal beauty, power and purpose. Now you realize that you no longer have to put up with negative thoughts about failing ever again. You just have to focus on looking at your magic mirror to know the right path and realize how your skills, beauty, power and strength can lead you to your dreams.

As you look further into the magic mirror, you see your past painful situations that hinder you from moving forward and they slowly dissolve before your eyes. You are no longer the weak, inadequate, small person you used to be. All the pain from your childhood and adulthood are all completely gone and they will no longer haunt you again. All your pain is gone and you are healed. You just have to remember how your magic mirror looks at things and do the same. The magic mirror is truly amazing. Now you know that whenever a person throws a negative comment on you, it will bounce right off of the magic mirror and thrown back into their throats. These negative people will never again hurt you and cause you pain.

Your magic mirror is created to help you achieve success in everything you do from this day forward. You will always bring your magic mirror in your mind to keep reminding yourself how brilliant, powerful, capable, beautiful, wonderful, successful and talented you are.

No one will ever hurt you again. Now that you know how awesome and amazing you are, you can achieve anything you want without getting hurt by negative feedbacks from negative people. You know you can do it and you believe that you can do it. Share your magic mirror with others and let them experience success like you do.

Chapter 6: The Benefits That You Gain From Visualization

Visualization is a mental rehearsal that helps you get more of what you want in life. Aside from helping you achieve success in life, visualization offers more benefits:

- Visualization helps you improve your self-image. When you impress successful images of yourself on your subconscious mind, you are also improving your self-image. It makes you feel more confident, happier and more capable.

- You get solutions to your problems when you visualize. When you visualize clearly and vividly, you experience insights that can help you get back on track whenever you are faced with difficulties and roadblocks on your way to success. When you visualize, you get hunches and ideas that can help you defeat your challenges.

- When you visualize, you produce new ideas, telling you what to do and how to do it.   All you need to do is put these ideas into practice.

- Visualization increases your focus and your desire to achieve your goal. When you are definite with your intent and you have the desire to turn it into reality, you are in the right track to success.

- Visualizing what you want in your life makes you feel relaxed and peaceful. It is the joy that it brings when you feel what it is like to live the life that you desire.

- When you imagine your dream life vividly in your mind, you eliminate conformism and fear and replace it with desire and possibility. Visualization gives you a sneak preview of yourself performing at your very best, making it good for the soul. It makes you feel replenished, gives you a higher sense of purpose and increases your energy.

- Visualization has been proven to work. Athletes and successful people make use of mental rehearsal to maximize their performance. Visualization prepares you for the real thing. The clearer and more vivid your visualizations are, you realize that your subconscious mind automatically takes over whenever you need to perform

You reap all of these benefits when you practice visualization. It helps you increase your performance and actually makes you healthier.

Conclusion

Thank you again for purchasing this book!

I hope this book was able to help you understand the visualization process and how you can use it to accomplish your plans.

Visualization is a powerful tool that helps you envision the life that you desire for yourself. In doing so, you are training your subconscious mind to make your body act the way it should when you need it to. Vividly visualizing yourself as the successful person that you desire helps improve the way you look at yourself, thereby increasing your confidence.

Since visualization helps you produce more ideas, it helps you improve your performance and boost your confidence, as well as, give you more focus and desire to achieve your end goal.

The next step is to get started on using these strategies and becoming who you dream to be!

If you know of anyone else that could benefit from the information presented here please inform them of this book.

Finally, if you enjoyed this book and feel it has added value to your life in any way, please take the time to share your thoughts and post a review on Amazon. It'd be greatly appreciated!

Thank you and good luck!

Preview Of:

<u>Overcome Fear</u>

Presentations And Speaking Guide To Overcome Fear And Shyness, Develop Self Confidence And Communication Skills, And Simply Talk To People!

Introduction

I want to thank you and congratulate you for purchasing the book, *"You Won't DIE Public Speaking - 5 Easy Steps To Overcome Anxiety And Be Great Public Speaking!"*

This book contains proven steps and strategies on how to overcome anxiety and nervousness while public speaking.

Your worst nightmare has come true, you just got a phone call from a friend of yours asking you to speak at her wedding as the maid of honor!!! Now what are you going to do? Just even the mere thought of doing this speech has got your hands starting to sweat and your heart beat racing.

You reluctantly agree and thank your friend for such an honor, but deep down inside you really wish you could somehow get out of this responsibility. You start asking yourself, is there an excuse I can come up with or some other way to tell my friend to ask someone else? You hurriedly get off the phone and begin to freak out!

If you have ever felt a feeling like this or similar to this, then you know exactly what it's like to have a fear of public speaking. Public speaking is one of the most feared things in our culture today. But why is it so scary, why do people have such a high amount of fear and anxiety towards speaking in public?

This book is going to help you overcome this fear and realize that there's really nothing to fear and all. By the time you finish the pages of this book I guarantee you that you will feel much better about your ability to speak in public, and not only that, you'll be eager to do so!

Thanks again for purchasing this book, I hope you enjoy it!

Chapter 1 – Public Speaking Essentials

"Fear and adrenaline are normal. When public speaking they are necessary! Without fear you would not prepare, and without adrenaline you would not have energy to move the crowd."

- Anonymous

Public speaking is a very broad concept, which has been considered a relevant human activity and skill for many centuries. Feudal lords, kings, rulers, conquerors, explorers, writers, artists, and innovators have used the power of words and gestures to win the hearts of many and overcome seemingly insurmountable obstacles. In the same way, you can utilize this instrument to show others that you can express yourself eloquently and confidently by speaking in front of a great audience.

Public Speaking is Unavoidable

Many people think that public speaking skills are not quite important because there are many instances wherein they can avoid addressing a crowd. This isn't really the case, though. As you'll soon realize—if you haven't observed it yet—public speaking is a part of daily life for most individuals. Even if your occupation or role in the academe doesn't necessarily require you to speak in front of many people on a daily basis, it's still important to be able to speak fluently and confidently.

Since it's unavoidable, learning how to carry yourself and be confident has consequently become a necessity. Confidence is an indispensable element in successful public speaking. If you want to succeed, you must have the guts to actually stand in front of an audience, no matter how small or large it may be. There will truly come a point in your life where you'll be asked to deliver a short or long message, so don't think you can just evade this possibility.

Fear is Normal

Learning and growth are impeded when fear dominates the mind and the heart. Fear is a constant companion of each and every individual and only those who have inaccurate perceptions of themselves think that they have never experienced being afraid of speaking in front of people. It's normal to be afraid because the mind uses a healthy dose of fear to warn the individual of the possible bad scenarios and the probability to fail.

People get nervous because what they're doing is important to them. More importantly, their image is quite valuable and they don't want to ruin it by messing up while speaking. Even great and famous public speakers or personalities get nervous when the spotlight's on them. Every moment on stage is unique because it's a whole new opportunity to either sweep the crowd off their feet or slip and fall through your words and excess nerves.

Once you accept the fact that fear is a normal part of public speaking, you can start growing. You can explore the next area of such an undertaking: what

constitutes your fear. Acceptance of the problem is the beginning of a great journey towards better public speaking skills. From here, you can have a better psychological setup.

What Scares You?

Fear of public speaking can stem from various elements, but in many cases, these causes are unfounded. Why? It's because they're just erroneously fabricated by a stressed mind. Your nervousness magnifies the negative, which certainly does not help clear your mind of unhelpful thoughts.

It's necessary to know what may or may not be scaring you because your anxieties or fears are not simple concerns, which you can just avoid by bottling every type of negativity up. The more you familiarize yourself with the things that prove to be adverse to your psychological condition, the better you can fight these fears off.

Thanks for Previewing My Exciting Book Entitled:

"Overcome Fear: Presentations And Speaking Guide To Overcome Fear And Shyness, Develop Self Confidence And Communication Skills, And Simply Talk To People!"

To purchase this book, simply go to the Amazon Kindle store and simply search:

"OVERCOME FEAR"

Then just scroll down until you see my book. You will know it is mine because you will see my name "Ryan Cooper" underneath the title.

Alternatively, you can visit my author page on Amazon to see this book and other work I have done. Thanks so much, and please don't forget your free bonuses

DON'T LEAVE YET! - YOUR FREE BONUSES ARE BELOW!

Free Bonus Offer 1: Get Free Access To The OperationAwesomeLife.com VIP Newsletter!

Free Bonus Offer 2: Get A Free Download Of My Friends Amazing Book "Passive Income" First Chapter!

Free Bonus Offer 3: Get A Free Email Series On Making Money Online When You Join Newsletter!

GET ALL 3 FREE

Once you enter your email address you will immediately get free access to this awesome **VIP NEWSLETTER**!

For a limited time, if you join for free right now, you will also get free access to the first chapter of the awesome book "**PASSIVE INCOME**"!

And, last but definitely not least, if you join the newsletter right now, you also will get a free 10 part email series on **10 SUCCESS SECRETS OF MAKING MONEY ONLINE!**

To claim all 3 of your FREE BONUSES just click below!

Just Go Here for all 3 VIP bonuses!

OperationAwesomeLife.com

Made in the USA
Middletown, DE
06 March 2019